FOLENS IDEAS BANK TUDOR TIMES

Peter Hepplewhite
Neil Tonge

Contents

How to use this book	2	Cures and remedies	24
Introduction	3	Crime and punishment	26
		Having a good time	28
Chronology card game	4	William Shakespeare	30
The Field of the Cloth of Gold	8	Town guilds	32
What do you think of Henry VIII?	10	Disgraceful apprentices	34
The break with Rome	12	Trade	36
Closing the monasteries and friaries	14	Seafarers in trouble	38
		The Spanish Armada	40
The Pilgrimage of Grace	16	Sir Francis Drake – hero or pirate?	42
The Church under Mary I	18	Power game	44
Plague streets	20	Tudor heritage	46
Rich and poor	22	Eight ways to help ...	48

How to use this book

Ideas Bank books provide you with ready to use, practical photocopiable activity pages for children **plus** a wealth of ideas for extension and development.

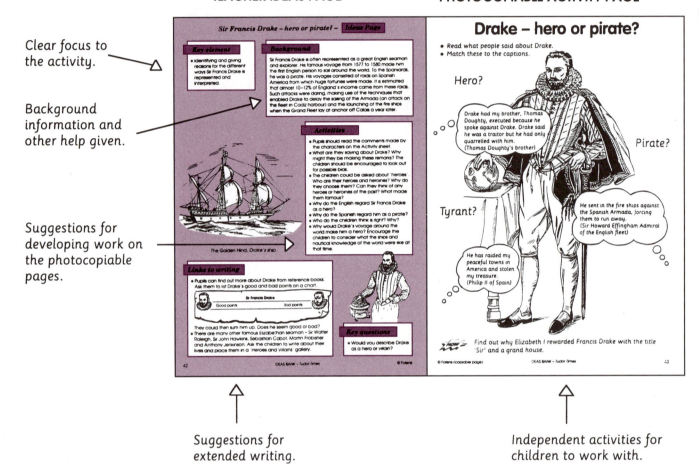

- Time-saving, relevant and practical, **Ideas Bank** books ensure that you will always have work ready at hand.

Folens allows photocopying of pages marked 'copiable page' for educational use, providing that this use is within the confines of the purchasing institution. Copiable pages should not be declared in any return in respect of any photocopying licence.

Folens books are protected by international copyright laws. All rights are reserved. The copyright of all materials in this book, except where otherwise stated, remains the property of the publisher and authors. No part of this publication may be reproduced, stored in a retrieval system, or transmitted, in any form or by any means, for whatever purpose, without the written permission of Folens Limited.

This resource may be used in a variety of ways. However, it is not intended that teachers or children should write directly into the book itself.

Peter Hepplewhite and Neil Tonge hereby assert their moral rights to be identified as the authors of this work in accordance with the Copyright, Designs and Patents Act 1988.

Editor: Alison Millar
Illustrations: Virginia Gray
Layout artist: Patricia Hollingsworth
Cover image: National Portrait Gallery, London

© 1996 Folens Limited, on behalf of the authors.

Every effort has been made to contact copyright holders of material used in this book. If any have been overlooked, we will be pleased to make any necessary arrangements.

First published 1996 by Folens Limited, Albert House, Apex Business Centre, Boscombe Road, Dunstable, LU5 4RL, England.

ISBN 1 85276871-1

Printed in Singapore by Craft Print.

Introduction

The Tudor dynasty came to the throne in 1485 when Henry VII defeated Richard III at the Battle of Bosworth. The crown passed to the Stuarts when Elizabeth I died without heirs in 1603.

The key political and religious event of the period was the Reformation – the split of the Christian Church into Catholics and Protestants. The main cause was Henry's need for a male heir to secure the Tudor family grip on the throne. Henry VIII dragged England into the Protestant camp to secure his divorce from Catherine of Aragon. He ruthlessly used his dispute with the Pope to create the Church of England with himself as its head in 1534. When he began to abolish the monasteries in 1536 he provoked one of the most serious rebellions of the time – the Pilgrimage of Grace. It was Henry's intent that the ordinary people would notice little change. He aimed to keep all the trappings of the Catholic Church, changing only the administrative structure. However, many of his subjects would have preferred to stay Catholic and it took a reign of terror to secure his rule.

Protestantism was strengthened during the brief reign of Edward VI (1547–1553) but its roots were not yet deep. Under Mary I (1553–1558) Catholicism and Papal authority returned. This was generally welcomed in spite of the burning of Protestant martyrs such as Bishops Latimer and Ridley. However, fate took a hand; Mary reigned for only five years before she died in 1558. Elizabeth I (1558–1603) attempted to find a compromise by restoring a moderate kind of Protestantism. However, stern measures were taken against practising Catholics after the Pope excommunicated Elizabeth in 1570 and Philip of Spain launched the Armada in 1588.

During the sixteenth century, England entered the race for overseas trade and colonies challenging the Spanish and the Dutch. Sir Francis Drake attacked Spanish treasure ships and, between 1577 and 1580, made his famous circumnavigation of the world. Sir Walter Raleigh claimed Virginia for his queen in 1585.

Tudor monarchs lived in great splendour and pageantry with the Court as the centre of complex power games. However, Tudor society was deeply divided. A walk down the street of any town showed enormous differences in standards of living, from great landowners to beggars. Although 90% of the population lived in the countryside, towns were centres of economic activity and wealth. Trades and crafts were controlled by guilds, with strict apprenticeship rules.

Life could be precarious. One fifth of all children died in the first year of life. Living conditions were grim, with filthy streets and open sewers making ideal breeding-grounds for the plague. Medical knowledge was little better than in the Middle-Ages, relying largely on herbal cures and remedies. Petty crime was widespread and dealt with by local magistrates, with punishments ranging from fines to severe whippings.

Entertainment for ordinary people could be rough and bloodthirsty, frequently involving cruelty to animals or other people, such as bear baiting or bare-knuckle boxing. However, both rich and poor enjoyed drama, including the often ribald Mystery plays of the Guilds and the work of professional playwrights, notably Shakespeare. His plays enjoyed royal patronage and were often propaganda for the Tudor monarchs.

The ideas in this book offer teachers a rich photocopiable resource, exploring the themes outlined above. Activities address the full range of key elements through a range of lively classroom tasks. These include questioning the motives of some of the main personalities, evaluating primary source material and decision-making based on appropriate background information.

Chronology card game – Ideas page

Key element

- Understanding the chronology of the Tudor monarchs.

Activities

- Provide the children with a copy of the Tudor fact file for reference. Photocopy and laminate three sets of the cards.
- The card game is for 4–6 players. Five cards are dealt to each player. The remaining cards are placed in a pile in the centre of the table. Players take turns to discard a card and pick up a replacement from the pile. The winner is the first player with a full set of Tudor monarchs.
- The children could also collect a run of three Tudor personalities.
- More able children could ask someone else for a card that they need. They are not allowed to ask for it directly (for instance, 'Have you got Henry VIII?'), but must ask for it obliquely (for instance, 'Have you got the card of the son of Henry VII?').
- Challenge groups of children to find portraits of other Tudors. They could draw them to extend the game. The greater the range of cards the more difficult it is to collect the set of monarchs.

Key question

- How could a person become a monarch?

Background

The Tudor monarchs ruled from 1485 to 1603 (the crown then passed to the Stuart family, on the death of Elizabeth I, because there were no Tudor heirs). England underwent considerable change during this period.

Monarchs possessed and exercised considerable power compared to the monarchy of today. They could pass laws, wage wars and give orders for the execution of individuals, as well as decide when parliaments should meet and when they had finished their business.

Links to writing

- Encourage the children to devise their own game based on the cards. They must provide clear instructions for the players.

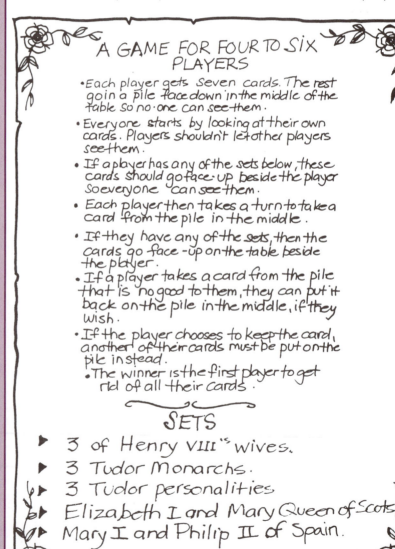

A GAME FOR FOUR TO SIX PLAYERS

- Each player gets seven cards. The rest go in a pile face down in the middle of the table so no-one can see them.
- Everyone starts by looking at their own cards. Players shouldn't let other players see them.
- If a player has any of the sets below, these cards should go face-up beside the player so everyone can see them.
- Each player then takes a turn to take a card from the pile in the middle.
- If they have any of the sets, then the cards go face-up on the table beside the player.
- If a player takes a card from the pile that is no good to them, they can put it back on the pile in the middle, if they wish.
- If the player chooses to keep the card, another of their cards must be put on the pile instead.
- The winner is the first player to get rid of all their cards.

SETS

▶ 3 of Henry VIII's wives.
▶ 3 Tudor Monarchs.
▶ 3 Tudor personalities
▶ Elizabeth I and Mary Queen of Scots
▶ Mary I and Philip II of Spain.

Chronology card game

Henry VII
1485–1509

Henry VIII
1509–1547

Edward VI
1547–1553

Mary I
1553–1558

Elizabeth I
1558–1603

Catherine of Aragon

Anne Boleyn

Philip II of Spain

Anne of Cleves

Chronology card game

Thomas More

Jane Seymour

Elizabeth of York

Mary Queen of Scots

Sir Walter Raleigh

Sir Francis Drake

Lady Jane Grey

Catherine Parr

Catherine Howard

IDEAS BANK – *Tudor Times*

Fact file

Henry VII 1485–1509
The first of the family of Tudor monarchs. He became king after defeating his enemy, Richard III, at the Battle of Bosworth.

Henry VIII 1509–1547
Henry married six times. He wanted a son who would rule after his death.

Edward VI 1547–1553
Henry VIII's only son from his six marriages. He became king before his elder sisters. He was a sickly boy and died at 16 years of age.

Mary I 1553–1558
She wanted to make England a Catholic country once more. Some important Protestant leaders were burned at the stake.

Elizabeth I 1558–1603
The last Tudor monarch. She never married so there were no children to continue the Tudor family.

Catherine of Aragon
Henry VIII's first wife and the mother of Mary I. Henry made himself head of the Church of England to divorce her and marry Anne Boleyn.

Anne Boleyn
Henry VIII's second wife and the mother of Elizabeth I. She was suspected of being unfaithful to Henry and was taken to the tower and beheaded.

Philip II of Spain
Ruler of Spain, the Netherlands, Milan and the New World. He married Mary I in 1554. The marriage was unpopular in England as he was Spanish and a Catholic.

Anne of Cleves
Henry VIII's fourth wife. Henry did not like her as she was neither beautiful nor musical (Henry loved music) and she agreed to a divorce.

Thomas More
Lord Chancellor of England for Henry VIII. He refused to give up his Roman Catholic beliefs and was beheaded.

Jane Seymour
Henry VIII's third wife. She gave birth to Henry's only son, Edward, who later became King Edward VI. Jane died shortly after his birth.

Elizabeth of York
Wife of Henry VII. This marriage brought together the warring families of York and Lancaster.

Mary Queen of Scots 1543–1567
Queen of Scotland but angered the Scots by her behaviour. Elizabeth I imprisoned her. She was eventually beheaded in Fotheringay Castle.

Sir Walter Raleigh
One of Elizabeth I's daring seamen. He began a colony in North America. He was later executed by James I.

Lady Jane Grey
The daughter-in-law of the Duke of Northumberland. He tried to make her queen instead of Mary, but she lasted only nine days before being beheaded.

Sir Francis Drake
One of Elizabeth I's most daring sailors who made raids on Spanish America and fought the Armada.

Catherine Howard
The fifth wife of Henry VIII. She was much younger than Henry. She was beheaded after being found guilty of having a love affair with another man.

Catherine Parr
The sixth wife of Henry VIII. She spoke many languages and was responsible for educating Mary and Elizabeth. She nursed Henry until he died in 1547.

The Field of the Cloth of Gold – Ideas Page

Key elements

- Understanding the relationships between English and other European monarchs.
- Analysing an important source related to the Field of the Cloth of Gold.

Activities

- Read the background information to the children. Challenge them to find pictures and accounts of this important diplomatic event.
- Discuss why Henry VIII might organise such a huge event. What were people meant to think about Henry?
- Can the children suggest how they might impress an important person visiting the school?
- Ask the children to find other examples of how monarchs impressed their subjects? How did they do it and on what occasions? How were objects and occasions meant to impress?
- Watch videos of present-day state occasions including politicians or monarchs. Can the children see any similarities between these and the Field of the Cloth of Gold? How do present day leaders try to impress each other?

Key question

- How did Tudor monarchs impress important people?

Background

Henry VIII, like other European monarchs, showed his power by spending money on ceremonies and pageantry. The 'Field of the Cloth of Gold' was a meeting between Henry VIII and Francis I of France outside the town of Guisnes, near Calais.

The monarch was expected to be generous with gifts and, in turn, subjects and ambassadors were meant to return the generosity.

The 'Field of the Cloth of Gold' lasted two weeks and was intended to symbolise France and England's reconciliation after centuries of mutual hatred and mistrust. Although the meeting seemed to go well, France and England were at war within two years of the meeting.

Clothing: Kings and queens were expected to show their importance by the way they dressed. Their clothes were often covered in gold thread and jewels.

Links to writing

- Ask the children to imagine they are an ambassador from an another European country. They have been asked by Henry VIII to prepare a meeting between himself and Charles V, the Holy Roman Emperor. The meeting is to take place in Germany.
  – What should the king wear for the occasion?
  – What soldiers should he take with him and how should they be dressed?
  – What musicians should be taken?
  – What servants will be needed?
  – What transport should be available?
- Once they have decided all these things the children should sketch a procession of who will be involved, in the order in which they will be presented to the Emperor.

The Field of the Cloth of Gold

This picture shows the 'Field of Cloth of Gold'. This was a meeting between the French king, Francis I and Henry VIII in 1520.

The dragon is meant to show a huge fireworks display.

The tents where the two kings met were made from gold cloth.

The fountain spurted real wine.

- How did Henry VIII try to impress Francis I and his court?

A palace was also built. It had brick foundations, wooden walls and real glass in the windows. Glass was very expensive.

How King Henry VIII tried to impress Francis I		
Expensive things	Modern things (in Tudor times)	Unusual things

- Why did they need to do this and where would they get the money from to pay for all these things?
  Why might this make some monarchs unpopular?
- If you had to plan an event that would impress someone important, what would you do?

What do you think of Henry VIII? – Ideas Page

Key element

- Introducing the concept of monarchy through interpreting the reign of Henry VIII.

Background

Historians have revised their views of Henry VIII. He is no longer seen as bluff king Hal defending English liberty against Catholic Europe. Now he is seen as a tyrant because of his execution of political enemies (around 70 000 out of a population of about five million). His desperate search for a son shows the insecurity of the Tudor dynasty. His father Henry VII had taken the crown at the battle of Bosworth in 1485. A crown won by the sword could be lost by the sword and Henry VIII was accutely aware that during the reign of the last female monarch in England, the county had been plunged into a bloody civil war.

1491 Henry VIII born. → 1509 Marriage to Catherine of Aragon. Coronation as Henry VIII. → 1513 Battle of Flodden. James IV of Scotland killed. → 1520 Meets Francis I at the Field of the Cloth of Gold. → 1533 Birth of Elizabeth I → 1534 Henry becomes Head of the Church of England.

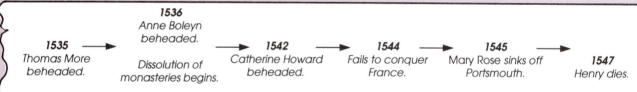

1535 Thomas More beheaded. → 1536 Anne Boleyn beheaded. Dissolution of monasteries begins. Catholic rebellion. → 1542 Catherine Howard beheaded. → 1544 Fails to conquer France. → 1545 Mary Rose sinks off Portsmouth. → 1547 Henry dies.

Activities

- Discuss what makes a good king or queen. What do good or bad rulers do in stories familiar to the children? How do they keep control?
- The children could draw up a job description for the position of Henry VIII. What skills and knowledge would he need to be a good ruler? What sort of character would a monarch have needed in 1509?

Job description for a king	
Age: between 21 and 60	
Skills needed:	**Knowledge needed:**
Ability to sort out quarrels	Warfare – fighting ships.
Arguing	What is going on all over England.
Archery	What is going on in Europe.
Character:	
Brave	How to impress people.
Strong	How to raise money for armies and ships.
Considerate	

Links to writing

- Research and write a chronicle of the life of Henry VIII. Display this as a large timeline or frieze.
- Divide the class into groups to find out about different aspects of the king (his wives, quarrel with the Pope, rebellion in 1536 and 1549, wars, court life, courtiers and so on).
- Prepare a list of Henry VIII's good and bad points. Make a final judgement on his reign with the title 'Henry VIII: My verdict on his reign'.

Key questions

- What makes a good ruler?
- Was Henry VIII a good ruler?

What do you think of Henry VIII?

- Historians argue about how good a king Henry VIII was. Read what Henry is saying here. Make lists of his good and bad points. Do you think he was a good or a bad king?

I married six times. I had two wives executed and divorced two.

My armies defeated the Scots at the battle of Flodden in 1513.

I tried to conquer France in 1544. My armies captured Boulogne, but were then driven out by French and Spanish troops.

When I was a young king, my court was a happy and lively place. I wrote fine poetry and music. I hunted and gave great feasts.

As I became old and fat, I grew ill and bad tempered.

I made England a Protestant country. English people had to obey me, not the Pope in Rome.

My wars cost a lot of money. To raise the cash, I put up taxes and sold the lands of the monasteries.

I needed a son to make England safe when I died. This was more important than any wife.

Many Catholics tried to stop me. They were traitors. I had thousands of enemies executed during my reign.

My people loved me. They were pleased to pay for my palaces and court.

- Find out about some of the things that Henry did that have affected present-day Britain.

The break with Rome – Ideas Page

Key element

- Understanding the range of conflicting points of view and the dilemmas faced by Roman Catholics during the reign of Henry VIII.

Henry badly wanted a son.

- Catherine of Aragon's only living child was a girl and she was too old to have any more children.
- Henry fell in love with Anne Boleyn who is younger and more likely to be able to have children.

Henry divorced Catherine and married Anne Boleyn.

Henry's divorce angered the Pope and Henry broke with Rome.

Background

There had been some concern for years over the power and wealth of the Catholic Church. Some church officials and leaders of monasteries had been found to be corrupt. Some members of religious orders were not keeping their vows of poverty, obedience and chastity. At first Henry tried to defend the Catholic Church in a book written against the critics. The Pope honoured Henry by giving him the title, 'Defender of the Faith'.

When the Pope refused to grant Henry a divorce, however, Henry turned to Protestant support. He wanted to retain the Catholic services while making himself Supreme Head of the Church in England. Then he would be able to grant himself a divorce. It was at this time that he began sending officials from his court to investigate the monasteries. They were instructed to look for examples of corruption.

Activities

- The children will need to be familiar with the terms 'Catholic' and 'Protestant'.
- The Activity sheet can be done as a group or by each child taking one of the characters (this would require further research).
- If the activity is carried out by individuals, there should be some discussion beforehand. A range of conclusions could be presented to the class.

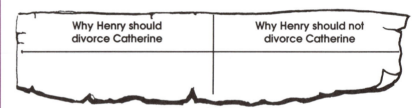

Why Henry should divorce Catherine	Why Henry should not divorce Catherine

- The background information could be presented to explain the actual decision and its effects.

Links to writing

- Explore the different methods of illustrating the relationship of causes, so that the children can see how events are interconnected. An example is illustrated above.
- Ask the children to write the causes of Henry's break with Rome on strips of paper and them arrange them in order of priority (for instance, 'Henry wanted a son', 'Henry loved Anne Boleyn' and so on).
- Encourage the children to consider why differing orders of events have arisen and whether this means one set of interpretations is better than another.

Key question

- Why did England break away from the Roman Catholic church?

The break with Rome

- Read these people's views of Henry VIII's divorce. Should he divorce his wife?

Henry VIII

"My only living child is a girl. I need a son."

Anne Boleyn

"Henry loves me. He wants to divorce Catherine and marry me."

Catherine of Aragon

"I am too old to have more children."

A Tudor man

"A female monarch will be weak."

The Pope

"Divorce is not allowed in the Roman Catholic Church. I will tell all the Catholic countries to fight you."

An English Protestant

"The Pope should not be head of the Church in England. I will support you."

Charles V Holy Roman Emperor

"I am a powerful ruler in Europe. Catherine is my aunt and if you try to divorce her, I will lead an attack on you."

Thomas Cranmer

"Your marriage to Catherine is unlawful. She was married to your dead brother, Arthur. It is wrong to marry your brother's widow."

Thomas More

"Although you are my king, I must obey the Pope."

- My advice to Henry is

_____

_____

_____

 • With friends, enact a scene between these characters.

Closing the monasteries and friaries – Ideas Page

Key element

- Helping children understand the range of points of view concerning the closure of the monasteries.

Background

The Church controlled about one quarter of all the land in England and its income was greater than that of Henry VIII. As the king had to raise revenue for himself, he was tempted to do so by confiscating church property, particularly after he had broken with Rome.

Henry sent commissioners to examine all the monasteries, nunneries and friaries to find out how well they were performing their duties. In January 1535 they visited about 800 monasteries and reported that many were lax in many ways. This gave Henry the evidence he needed. In 1536 an Act of Parliament ordered the closure of all small monasteries, and in 1539 all the larger monasteries were closed. Most monks, nuns and friars were pensioned off with many becoming parish priests or teachers; the few abbots who opposed the closure were hanged.

Activities

- Read the 'Ten sins of monks' aloud. These were all the things which monks, nuns and friars were not supposed to do.
- The people on the Activity sheet each have two main considerations regarding the closure of religious houses. The children should decide what the people will say. They then count up those who support the closure and those who are opposed to it. What is the overall decision?
- The roles of the characters could be acted out by members of each group and a joint decision made on the basis of listening to each other's arguments.

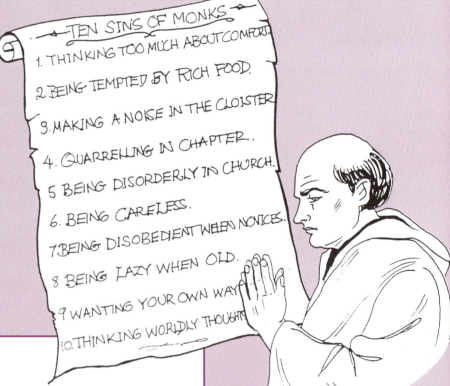

Links to writing

- The children could write a script for a play which is based on the following scenario:
  Guildsmen and monks work on an Easter production of a mystery play, such as 'Noah's Flood'. The guildsmen enact the play whilst the friars provide the service of thanksgiving. A commissioner arrives. The commissioner questions the friars and deliberately misinterprets their answers. The commissioner then asks the guildsmen for their views; they are sympathetic to the friars and the commissioner reminds them that he is on the king's instructions and it is treason to oppose the king. He might also offer the friars a pension.
- The children should decide the ending – what will the friars and the guildsmen do?

Key questions

- Why did Henry VIII want to close the monasteries?
- Who else would benefit if they were closed?

Should the friary be closed?

Henry VIII wanted to close down friaries and monasteries.
- Read what these people are thinking and then decide whether they would agree to the closing of the friary.

The friars help poor people, but we need a new meeting place for the guild. The old friary will be useful if the king sells it to us.

The guildsman

I must only find things that are honestly wrong in the friary, but the king wants the friaries to close.

Commissioner Ascham

I am in charge of the friary and must obey the Pope. I must also obey the king who is now head of the Church of England.

I wish to remain a friar, but I could become a parish priest.

Brother Dominic

Friar Godwin

The Merchant

I have given gifts to the friary so that the monks will pray for me when I am dead. We can give them a pension so they won't starve.

- What will happen to the friary? Explain your answer.

_____
_____
_____
_____

 • Find out about the work of nuns and monks. Write a letter to Henry VIII as if you were one, explaining why a friary should stay open.

The Pilgrimage of Grace – Ideas Page

Key elements

- Developing an understanding of the characteristic features of religious conflict of the period.
- Studying the reasons for the Pilgrimage of Grace and its results.

Background

Henry created the Church of England for personal reasons, not in response to popular demand. Research now indicates that many people were happy with the Catholic Church. The Reformation, as it came to be known, was introduced piecemeal, over a decade and few realised what was happening until it was too late.

The dissolution of the monasteries in 1536 did, however, provoke resistance. It affected many lay people, especially those employed or aided by the monks. In the north, about 40 000 joined the Pilgrimage of Grace, led by Robert Aske. Henry persuaded them to go home by promising that their monasteries would be spared. When they dispersed, troops executed many pilgrims.

Other Catholics hoped to sit out the Reformation. A priest in London in 1536 gave the following advice to those worried about choosing between Pope and king:

> Be comforted. Do not give up your faith and God will reward us even more. These things will not last long. You will see the world change again.

A priest in London gave advice to those worried about choosing between the Pope and Henry VIII.

Links to writing

- Ask the children what they think a pilgrim might write in a letter to their family.
- What might the final message of a pilgrim be? The children could write a short passage or message that could be carved on a prison wall. Many pilgrims would have been illiterate so the message could be in a pictorial format.

Activities

- Think about the words 'pilgrim' and 'grace'. Do the children think this is a good name for the rebels? Discuss why the pilgrims might take an oath and how this might make them better soldiers.
- Why were many Catholics unwilling to rebel? What would the dangers be? The children should think about the difficulties of choosing between king and Pope. They could list these difficulties on a chart.

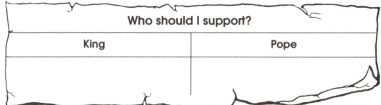

| Who should I support? ||
King	Pope

- Visit modern-day Protestant and Catholic churches. Find out about the differences and similarities in the faiths now.

This is a picture of a stone carving done by an illiterate pilgrim while imprisoned in Warkworth Castle. It is thought to show the crucified Christ and the heads of the apostles.

Key questions

- How did people feel about the Reformation?
- Why did some Catholics rebel?

Pilgrims of Grace

In 1536 Robert Aske led a rebellion in the north of England. The rebels were Catholics who wanted to stop Henry VIII closing monasteries. They called their fight the 'Pilgrimage of Grace'.

Glossary	
alms	money to keep people in need
heretics	people who supported the new Church in England

Source A

You will not join our Pilgrimage for your own profit. You will not kill or hurt anyone unless you are ordered to. You will not be afraid, for before you goes the Cross of Christ. We fight to protect the Church and defeat the heretics.

An oath drawn up by Robert Aske for his followers, 1536.

Source B

I did object to the closing of the monasteries and so did all the country. In the north they gave alms to the poor and served God well. Such abbeys were one of the beauties of this country to all men. They looked after and built sea walls, bridges and highways.

Robert Aske, from the Tower of London, 1537.

- Look at source A. Make a list of three things that Robert Aske's men must promise not to do. Why do you think he wants them to behave well?

- Look at source B. What reasons does Robert Aske give for defending the monasteries?

- Some Pilgrims were put in prison in Warkworth Castle, Northumberland. They carved pictures like these on the walls. Why might they have done this?

The Church under Mary I – Ideas Page

Key elements

- Identifying reasons for the way in which Mary Tudor is represented.
- Analysing sources upon which this interpretation is based.

Background

Edward VI, Henry VIII's son by Jane Seymour, ruled with the help of the Dukes of Somerset and Northumberland. His short reign continued Henry's reform of the English Church as a Protestant Church. He died in 1553 at the age of 16 and Mary I succeeded him as queen.

Mary was the eldest child of Henry VIII. Her mother was Catherine of Aragon who brought her up as a Roman Catholic. After becoming queen, she married Philip II of Spain, a powerful Roman Catholic.

Mary I was determined to make England Catholic once more. Church services were read in Latin, married priests had to leave their wives or give up their jobs and the Pope was restored as head of the English Church.

Many people did not want to see the English Church return to 'papism' and hoped that Mary would be deposed and that her Protestant sister, Elizabeth, would become queen instead. Some Protestants refused to accept the return of the Catholic faith and 273 were burned to death. Their names were recorded by John Foxe in his 'Booke of Martyrs'. Protestants nicknamed her 'Bloody Mary'.

Activities

- Supply the children with a brief background to the reign of Mary, particularly the use of the nickname 'Bloody Mary'.
- The children should then answer the questions on the Activity sheet and come to a view about whether the nickname is justified.
- Consider modern examples of people who have nicknames. What different types can the children think of? How have they got a particular nickname? Do they deserve it?
- Can the children explain why Foxe's *Booke of Martyrs* does not list the Catholic martyrs killed during the reigns of Henry VIII and Edward VI?

Links to writing

- Tell the children to imagine that the Pope has sent them from Rome in Italy to England. They should write a report to the Pope, explaining how Mary is helping to rid England of Protestants.
- Ask the children to write a prayer or poem, imagining that they are preparing to meet their death at the hands of Mary's executioners.

Key question

- How did Mary Tudor get the name of 'Bloody Mary'?

Mary I and the Church

Mary was a Roman Catholic.
- Use the sources to answer the questions.

Glossary
lyfe — life
wishte — wished

Source A

Protestant bishops Latimer and Ridley being executed. From the Booke of Martyrs, by John Foxe.

Source B

A coin that was made just after the death of Mary. The Pope with an important churchman. The words mean (left) 'An evil church has the face of the devil' and (right) 'Sometimes wise men, sometimes foolish'.

Source C

When William Allen at Walsingham
For truth was tried in fiery flame
When Roger Cooe, that good old man,
Did lose his lyfe for Christ's name;
When these others were put to death,
We wishte for our Elizabeth.

An old rhyme.

- Why did Mary have Protestants burned in public?

- Who did some people want as queen instead of Mary?

- Which people wished for Elizabeth and why?

- Turn Source B upside-down. What do you see? Was it made by Catholics or Protestants? Explain your answer.

- Imagine you are a Protestant living at the time of Mary I. Write a letter to a friend describing your feelings. Explain why you might want Elizabeth (Mary I's younger half-sister) to be Queen instead of Mary.

Plague streets – Ideas Page

Key element

- Appreciating the unhealthy living conditions in Tudor towns and how these resulted in repeated outbreaks of bubonic plague.

People tried to protect themselves from the plague by wearing masks and heavy clothing.

Background

Tudor towns could be grim, with small dark houses, unpaved narrow streets and open sewers (if there was any drainage at all). Rubbish strewn in the thoroughfares might consist of the offal from slaughtered animals, as well as human and animal excrement. Rats and parasites were plentiful.

Bubonic plague was endemic, with severe outbreaks recorded in 1516, 1528, 1545 and 1570. Often called the 'sweating sickness', symptoms included headaches, chill, delirium, black and red blotches on the skin and painful, pus-filled boils under the arms or in the groin. People didn't know then what caused the plague, though dirt was suspected. Prevention often amounted to using masks and perfumes to combat the foul smells from the streets. Occasionally, the streets were cleaned.

Activities

- Discuss how the seasons might affect conditions in towns. What would happen to unpaved streets in the rain? Would winter make the town a healthier place to be?
- Ask the children to research the plague. How did people try to stop it from spreading? What cures did they try and why did it keep coming back? Why don't people in Britain suffer from the plague now?
- Invite an environmental health officer to talk about modern health hazards including rats.

Links to writing

- Ask the children to draw up a list of town by-laws to put an end to the health hazards in the picture. They could begin 'By order of the Mayor, the people of ... shall forthwith cease the following practices:'.

Key questions

- What were the conditions like in Tudor towns?
- How did these conditions help spread the plague?

IDEAS BANK – *Tudor Times*

© Folens Ltd

Plague streets

Streets in Tudor towns were busy, noisy and dirty places. The unhealthy conditions caused the spread of diseases. The most frightening was the plague. People caught this from fleas carried by rats.

- Look carefully at the picture. List the health hazards.

   • Compare these health hazards with those of a present-day town.

Rich and poor – Ideas Page

Key element

- Using primary evidence to learn about the lives of people from different levels of Tudor society.

Activities

- The children work in pairs to role-play the scene. Once they have decided what is happening in the picture they should stand in the same postures as the characters and act out the scene, adding a happy and an unhappy ending (for example, the rich man offers the beggar a job on his farm, or the beggar is punished as a 'vagabond').
- Ask the children to draw the scene. This could be extended to a comic strip adventure in which the beggar tells the story of how he was forced to leave his land.
- Historians think the following well-known nursery rhyme originates from the sixteenth century:
  Hark, Hark
  the dogs do bark,
  The beggars are coming to town.
  Some in rags,
  And some in jags (tattered clothes),
  And one in a velvet gown.
  Discuss what it suggests about the Tudor attitude to vagrants – a source of fear or fun?
- The children could act out a scene where they are members of a town council. Will they ban beggars? They should suggest arguments for and against the motion.

Background

Possibly the greatest achievement of the Tudor age was to grow enough food for a rising population. However, this had a cost. Land had been cultivated using the medieval method of strips in communal fields, surrounded by common areas. Wealthy Tudor landowners began to enclose the common areas to increase production and profit, at the expense of traditional rights for poorer families such as free grazing.

Some poorer people became landless labourers, while others took to the roads in search of work. Many resorted to begging in the towns.

Fear of attack by beggars meant they were often treated harshly if they didn't move on. A whipping or time in the stocks were common punishments.

From regulations made at Chester in 1539

Links to writing

- Encourage the children to discuss the picture in detail. Which is the rich man and which is the poor man? How can they tell? Is the poor man begging or threatening? Is the rich man worried? Why isn't he looking at the beggar?
- They should fill in the speech and thought bubbles. Why might the characters not say out loud what they are thinking?

Key questions

- Who were the very poor and how were they treated?
- Why were beggars a problem in Tudor towns?

Rich and poor

This Tudor picture shows a rich man and a poor man.
What do you think is happening? What might they be saying to each other? What might they be thinking but not wanting to say?
- Fill in the thought bubbles and speech bubbles for each person.
- Describe the clothing each man is wearing.

_____
_____
_____

 • What happens next? Draw a cartoon strip to tell the story.

Cures and remedies – Ideas Page

Key elements

- Appreciating the extent of people's medical knowledge in Tudor times.
- Describing the changes in medical practice between Tudor times and the present day.

Background

Medical knowledge had changed little since medieval times: balancing the four 'humours' in the body (Earth, Air, Fire and Water). It was believed that illness was due to an imbalance of these.

Humours could be balanced in several ways, including bleeding of a patient by a surgeon who opened a vein by using cupping glasses or applying leeches. There was, of course, no anaesthetic or antiseptic. Apothecaries, or chemists, acted as doctors too, using herbal cures. Barbers performed operations and bled people.

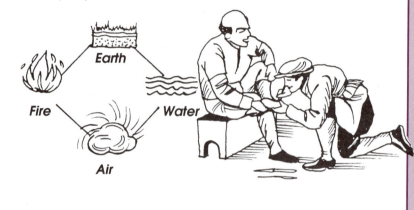

Activities

- Explain to the children medical knowledge during Tudor times and the Ancient Greek idea of the four humours, as shown in the diagram.
- Divide the class into groups and ask them to match the remedies to the diseases.
  Answers:

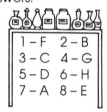

  1 – F   2 – B
  3 – C   4 – G
  5 – D   6 – H
  7 – A   8 – E

- The children could research other remedies to add them to a frieze of an apothecary's shop.
- Discuss what most of these remedies have in common. Why did the Tudors rely on such remedies to cure illness?
- In Tudor times there were no vaccinations and many illnesses, such as the plague, were incurable. Ask the children to list modern illnesses that are curable and incurable and those preventable by vaccination.
- Are there some Tudor illnesses that still exist today?

Links to writing

- The children could write a doctor's diary. They should imagine that they have to visit a number of patients over several days. All have different illnesses. They should keep a note of what remedies they suggest.

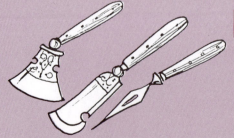

Tudor surgical instruments

Key questions

- Which of the complaints affect present-day people? Which do not?
- Are there any ways in which people still use herbal remedies?

Cures and remedies

The apothecary's apprentice cannot remember which treatment goes with which complaint.

• Write each complaint below the correct treatment and save the apprentice from a beating.

A
Shave the head and smear with the grease of a fox. If this fails, wash the scalp with the juice of beetles. If this still does not work, crush garlic, rub it in the head and wash in vinegar.

B  Drink a mixture of lavender, bay, rue, roses, sage and marjoram. If this does not work, press a hangman's rope to your head.

C Boil a red-haired dog in oil, add worms, pigs marrow and herbs. Make a mixture and put it on the swollen foot.

D Wear the skin of a donkey.

E Take the gall bladder (all food passes through this organ) of a hare and the grease of a fox. Warm the mixture and place in the ear.

F Cut open the swellings and place a mixture of fat and honey on the wound.

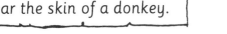

G Put tobacco juice on your head.

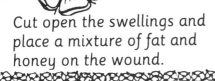

 H Swallow nine lice in a pint of ale every morning.

| 1. Plague | 2. Headache | 3. Gout | 4. Baldness |
| 5. Rheumatism | 6. Jaundice | 7. Headlice | 8. Deafness |

• Which of these complaints do people still suffer from?
• Find out how they are treated.

© Folens (copiable page)   IDEAS BANK – *Tudor Times*   25

Crime and punishment – Ideas Page

Key elements

- Explaining Tudor crimes and punishments.
- Understanding the reasons for and consequences of crime in Tudor times.

Background

During the Middle Ages, Justices of the Peace (magistrates) became increasingly responsible for local law and order. Crime records for the period are patchy and it is difficult to draw a national picture. The most recorded crime was theft, usually committed by people in need of food and clothing. Such crimes peaked at times of famine and unemployment.

Punishments could be harsh, for instance, whipping. However, fines and compensation payments were common. The stocks and the pillory were forms of public humiliation. The ducking stool was usually reserved for women.

The crimes on the Activity sheet have been readapted from Durham quarter sessions and are descriptions of real crimes that took place during the Tudor period. Although not recorded, the punishments were typical of the period.

Activities

- Ask the children to look at the different punishments. They should cut out the pictures and rank them in order, from least to most severe, explaining the order, especially the first and last.
- In pairs, they should choose one criminal and then discuss what questions a JP might want to ask before passing sentence. Write these down and share the ideas in a class discussion.
- Ask the children to bring in newspapers and look for reports of magistrates' courts. What differences and similarities can the children see between modern crimes and those on the Activity sheet?

A criminal is whipped round the town.

Fines	Irons	Ducking stool	Pillory	Whipping
1	2	3	4	5
Least severe punishment				Most severe punishment

Links to writing

- Discuss which punishments would be suitable for which crime. For example:

Name	Crime	Punishment
John Drummell	Stole a sheep	Stocks
Cuthbert Spence	Burglary	Stocks

Key questions

- What crimes were common in Tudor times? How were they punished?
- Why were these crimes common?

Crime and punishment

a) The pillory

Here are some common punishments from Tudor times.
- If you were a Justice of the Peace, how would you punish the criminals? You do not have to use every punishment.

b) The ducking stool

c) Whipping around the town

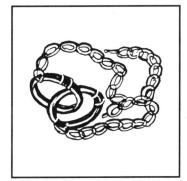
d) Irons

e) Fines

Criminal and crime	Punishment
John Drummell stole a sheep worth 10d (4p) from an unknown person.	
Cuthbert Spence, a joiner, burst open the house door of Christopher Hutchinson and stole two hats and a linen sheet worth 3s (15p).	
Laurence Hayle assaulted Richard Spurner, a queen's constable.	
Robert Bee bullied his neighbours and caused arguments.	
John Robinson made and sold shoes without serving an apprenticeship of seven years.	
Elizabeth Slater, a single woman, broke and entered the house of John Cokden and stole a woman's gown worth 40s (£2) and 11s (55p) in coins.	

- Explain your choice of punishments.
- List the punishments that you did not use. Are there crimes you would use them for? What are they?
- What might a Justice of the Peace want to know about each person before passing sentence. How might this affect the kind of punishment given?

© Folens (copiable page)   IDEAS BANK – Tudor Times

Having a good time – Ideas Page

Key element

- Helping the children to understand how people from different levels of Tudor society entertained themselves and how ideas of acceptable entertainment have changed since then.

Background

Life for most people meant hard physical work and time off for leisure was precious. Since communications were difficult, entertainment was largely local and traditional.

Many pastimes seem rough or bloodthirsty compared to today. The physical suffering of animals was enjoyed with relish and bear- and bull-baiting, hare-coursing and cock-and dog-fighting were very popular. The nobility enjoyed hunting deer, wild boar and birds of all kinds. Sports included cudgel play, wrestling and bare-knuckle boxing; football was little more than a running fist fight. A special treat might consist of attending a public execution.

More peaceful activities included bowls and skittles, draughts and chess, singing and dancing and listening to music. Touring bands of actors, jugglers and acrobats found plenty of work at market days and fairs around the country.

Activities

- Set the children a picture research task – they should find as many contemporary pictures of entertainments as possible and use them to prepare a frieze of a Tudor fair. Include the pastimes mentioned in the Background information.
- Discuss how attitudes to animals have changed. The children could make a chart to show how animals are used in sports today.

Animals for entertainment

Animals	Event or place
lion	circus
elephant	circus
horse	racing
dog	racing and circus

Links to writing

- The children could describe a village football match. The ball would be a stuffed pig's bladder, the rules simple – players start in the middle of the village and have to get the ball to either end. How might the weather affect play? The game is rough; who gets hurt? How? Who does the game annoy? Use the primary source below for inspiration.

> As for football playing, it may rather be called a friendly kind of fight. For doth not everyone lie in wait for his enemy, seeking to trip him and drop him on his nose, though it be on hard stones or in a ditch? Sometimes their necks are broken, sometimes their backs, sometimes their noses gush with blood.
>
> Philip Stubbes, Anatomie of Abuses, 1593.

Key question

- How did ordinary people enjoy themselves?

IDEAS BANK – *Tudor Times*

Having a good time

The pictures show how Tudor people enjoyed themselves in their leisure time.

- Look at the pictures and complete the chart.

Bear-baiting

Dancing

Watching plays

Cock-fighting

Tennis

Chess

Archery

Activity	Does it still take place?	Changes
1. Bear-baiting		
2. Dancing		
3. Watching plays		
4. Cock-fighting		
5. Tennis		
6. Chess		
7. Archery		

- Find out about some more Tudor pastimes. Describe who took part in them – men, women, boys, girls, rich or poor?

William Shakespeare – *Ideas Page*

Key elements

- Learning about cultural and political aspects of Tudor times.
- How drama was used to interpret past and current people and events.

Background

Drama was a popular entertainment for the rich and poor. In 1576 the first two purpose-built playhouses were opened in London. The theatre most closely associated with Shakespeare, the Globe, was opened in 1599.

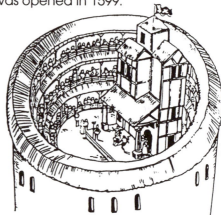

Most people could not read or write and plays were powerful ways of spreading ideas. New plays had to have approval from the Lord Chancellor before they could be performed.

Shakespeare became the most successful dramatist of his era, partly because his company, the Queen's Men, had the patronage of the court. In return he was expected to support the Tudor dynasty. In *Richard III*, the last Yorkist king is shown as a cruel, deformed, murdering tyrant.

In the extract from *Richard II* on this page, Shakespeare paints a glowing picture of England.

Activities

- Work through the extract on the Activity sheet line by line, underlining the key words which build up the picture of an evil man.
- Hold an evil-face-pulling contest.
- The children could also consider *Richard II*. (See the extract on this page.)
- Why did Shakespeare write about England in this way?

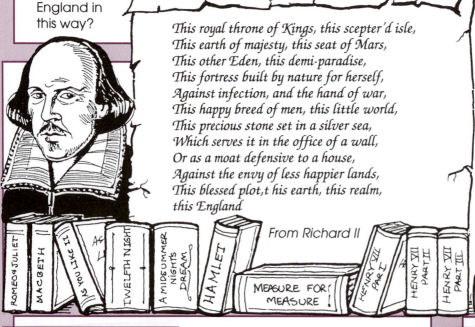

*This royal throne of Kings, this scepter'd isle,
This earth of majesty, this seat of Mars,
This other Eden, this demi-paradise,
This fortress built by nature for herself,
Against infection, and the hand of war,
This happy breed of men, this little world,
This precious stone set in a silver sea,
Which serves it in the office of a wall,
Or as a moat defensive to a house,
Against the envy of less happier lands,
This blessed plot, this earth, this realm, this England*

From *Richard II*

Links to writing

- Encourage the children to give a grim description of Richard III in their own words. They should make him a real villain. Brainstorm words.
- Historians now think Richard III was an able king. He was probably not deformed. Ask the children to describe Richard III as a noble, handsome and brave king. Would he like war? What would be spend his time thinking about?

Key questions

- Why did Shakespeare write so harshly about Richard III?
- Why would the Lord Chancellor want to control what was shown in plays?

William Shakespeare

Elizabeth I paid Shakespeare and his company of actors. They had to make sure that their plays would please her.

- Use the sources on this page to help you answer the questions.

Glossary

feature	normal shape
dissembling	disguising (Richard fooling himself into thinking that he is a good man inside)
halt	limp
weak piping time of peace	pipes of peace (Richard really wants war)
descant	talk

1. I that am ...
   Cheated of feature by dissembling nature,
   Deformed, unfinished, sent before my time,
   Into this breathing world scarce half made up,
5. And that so lamely and unfashionable
   That dogs bark at me as I halt by them
   Why I, in this weak piping time of peace,
   Have no delight to pass away the time,
   Unless to spy my shadow in the sun
10. And descant on mine own deformity.

Source A: some words from Richard III.

Fact file

Shakespeare wrote Richard III in 1592. Richard III had been killed at the Battle of Bosworth in 1485 by Henry VII, Elizabeth I's grandfather.

Source B

- Describe Richard III in your own words using source A.

- Would Elizabeth have liked your description? Explain your answer using source B.

- **NOW** • What do you think Richard III was really like?

Town guilds – Ideas Page

Key element

- Awareness of the importance of craft guilds in Tudor town life by using guild coats of arms as a source for historical enquiry.

A guild hall

Background

Most guilds or companies were formed during the Medieval or Tudor periods. In return for guaranteeing standards and supplies to consumers, the guilds were granted a local monopoly of trade. Non-members could not set up in competition. Each guild set wages, working hours and prices, regulated standards of manufacture and trained apprentices. Each also had its own elaborate coat of arms.

The guilds' influence extended into other areas of town life – its members often became mayors, sheriffs or council members. Social obligations included paying priests to pray for the welfare of the community and souls of the dead, organising Corpus Christi plays and looking after the poor.

Each guild had it's own coat of arms.

Saddlers Joiners Smiths

Butchers Masons Masters and Mariners

Activities

- Discuss the designs shown on the Activity sheet. How do they symbolise the guilds (for example, by showing the tools, products and raw materials connected with the guild)?
- Towns like Southampton, Bedford, London, Norwich, York and Newcastle had guilds. If a town in the school's locality was thriving in the Tudor period it probably had its own guild. The local studies library or archives will be able to help the children research these guilds. What trades did they cover? What were their rules and what did their coat of arms look like?

Key questions

- What impact did craft guilds have on Tudor life?
- What is the present-day equivalent of a guild?

Links to writing

- Ask the children to work out a set of rules for a guild. They should include items on workmanship, apprentices and contributing to the life of the town. The Guild of Masons in Newcastle was founded in 1581 and their rules included:

> *During the Corpus Christi plays to play The burial of Our Lady St Mary the Virgin. Any brother not taking part to pay 2s 6d. No one to take a Scotsman as an apprentice or pay a penalty of 40s. No Scot to be allowed to join the guild. Half of all fines to go to maintain the great bridge. All apprentices to serve seven years and to serve their masters dutifully.*

Town guilds

Guilds were groups of shopkeepers or craftspeople who did the same job. The three below belonged to guilds in Newcastle upon Tyne.

- Fill in the original colours on each coat of arms.

MASTERS AND MARINERS
Crest: gold ship.
Arms (shield): gold chain, boatswain's whistle and anchor top on blue background, rest of anchor blue on silver background.

MASONS
Crest: silver tower.
Arms (shield): silver towers on a black background, black compasses on a silver chevron (stripe).

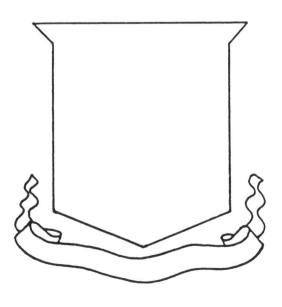

JOINERS
Crest: savage wearing green leaves at head and waist, holding a golden spear.
Arms (shield): red roses on gold background, silver shell on blue background, golden compasses and globe on red background, silver chevron (stripe).

- Use reference books to find out about the other guilds.
- On the blank shield design a coat of arms for smiths, saddlers or butchers.

Disgraceful apprentices – Ideas Page

Key element

- Understanding the term 'apprenticeship' and use contemporary documents for historical enquiry.

Background

The apprentice system was the core of industrial and commercial training. Guild masters, sometimes for a fee, agreed to teach young people their craft or occupation. Apprenticeships traditionally lasted seven years, starting from the age of 14. The custom of coming of age at 21 is partly based on the time when training finished.

Apprentices, usually boys (except in the woollen industry), normally became part of the master's household. They had to obey him and promise not to give away his business secrets. Guilds would usually only accept apprentices from well-to-do families, perhaps the sons of freemen of the town.

Concern about the behaviour of apprentices is a common theme in Guild records. Their behaviour could degenerate into drunken riots. The punishments ordered by the Newcastle Merchants' Guild were severe. Its order book lists important decisions made by the Guild. It was, in effect, a rule book.

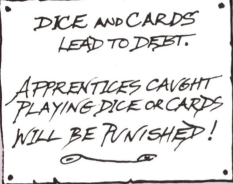

DICE AND CARDS LEAD TO DEBT.

APPRENTICES CAUGHT PLAYING DICE OR CARDS WILL BE PUNISHED!

Apprentices were forbidden to dance, dice, card or mum (act), use gitterns (guitars), wear cut hose, padded jerkins or wear a beard.

Activities

- Discuss the document on the Activity sheet in detail. When was it written? What was an order book? Why was it written? Why are the Masters so concerned about the behaviour of the apprentices? How might this affect their image in the town?
- Ask the children to write a paragraph describing the source with a brief summary of the contents. They could give this the title: Disgraceful apprentices – Explaining the Document.
- Look at place names in a town in your locality. What do they tell you about trades that were based there? The children could look at street maps to collect information. They could use computer software to construct a 'layered' database showing occupations in Tudor times and today.
- The children could draw a poster warning apprentices to change their ways. It could be captioned with a point of view from the Guild, for instance, 'Dice and cards lead to debt', or threatening punishment.

Links to writing

- In the letter task on the Activity sheet, the children might try to explain why apprentices need to enjoy themselves and how their behaviour may be thought of as harmless fun.
- List any unusual words.

Key questions

- How did young people behave in Tudor times?
- How did this behaviour annoy their elders?

Disgraceful apprentices

Apprentices were young people learning trades.
- Read the source and answer the questions.

Glossary

reverence	respect	gittern	guitar
mumming	acting	jerkin	short jacket
jagged hose	sort of tights lined with silk	housewife's cloth	plain cloth

In the past, the bringing up of apprentices was carried out by an elder with much care. Apprentices knew their duty. They showed reverence to the Master, obeyed their betters and were modest in eating, drinking and apparel.

But now there is disgraceful behaviour amongst those serving in the Guild. Who is to blame? Do we Masters no longer set an example by our good lives and words or are the apprentices lazy and stubborn?

In these days there is so much playing of dice, cards and mumming, with drinking, dancing, coats trimmed with decoration, jagged hose, use of gitterns, wearing beards and daggers worn slung across the back. This behaviour is more fitting to raging ruffians than honest apprentices.

So it is ordered by Cuthbert Ellison, Governor of this Guild, that no master will allow his apprentice to dance, dice, card or mum, use gitterns, wear cut hose, padded jerkins or wear a beard. His hose to be plain, of cheap cloth, and his coats of course cloth, of housewife's making. Any Master allowing his apprentice to break these rules shall pay the Guild 40 shillings (£2). The apprentice shall lose those years he has already served.

From the Merchant Venturers Charter and Act Book, Newcastle upon Tyne, 14th November 1554.

- What were the apprentices doing that the elders did not approve of?

- What was done to control the apprentices?

- If you were a Tudor apprentice, what would you think about this order? Write a letter to Cuthbert Ellison beginning 'Most Worshipful Sir, I beg you to think again'. Sign it 'Your Most Humble Servant'.

© Folens (copiable page)   IDEAS BANK – *Tudor Times*

Trade – Ideas Page

Key elements

- Understanding the importance of trade in this period.
- Knowing which items of trade were important and which countries Britain traded with.

Background

From the late 1400s onwards, Europeans made use of improvements in shipbuilding and navigation to find new routes to the Spice Islands east of India. England lagged behind Spain, France and Holland in this, but by the early Stuart period had established trading stations and colonies in North America and India. These trading outposts were the seeds of an empire that was to flower in the eighteenth and nineteenth centuries.

Britain exported its staple products of wool, woollen cloth, metals and grain. The industrial revolution grew from these industries, later enabling Britain to occupy a commanding position in the world.

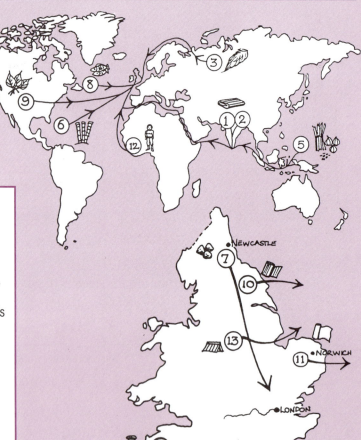

These maps show Britain's main imports and exports

Activities

- The scene is set in Bristol. Ask the children about ports. What happens in a port? Introduce the words 'exports' and 'imports'.
- Talk about the goods on the dock. Which parts of the world are they going to? What is being brought to England?
- Find out where the exports will be delivered to and where the imports are being sent to. Using a world map, trace the routes along which these goods would travel. What distances are involved?
- All goods had to be carried in sailing ships. Sailing ships could average about one hundred miles a day. How long would it take to reach some of the destinations?
- What difficulties would sailing ships meet?

Links to writing

- Why is there more trade today compared with the reign of Queen Elizabeth I? Ask the children to list the reasons.
- Encourage the children to write a time letter to her majesty explaining why trade has grown so much.

Key question

- What were the important items of trade during the Tudor period?

Trade

This is Bristol in 1603. The goods have become mixed up on the dock.
• Which goods are exports and which are imports? Sort them out and load them on to the right ship. Link them to the ships with lines.

1. SALTPETRE from INDIA
2. COTTON from INDIA
3. FURS from RUSSIA
4. TIN from CORNWALL
5. SPICES from EAST INDIES
6. SUGAR CANE from WEST INDIES
7. COAL from NORTH-EAST ENGLAND
8. SALTED FISH from NEWFOUNDLAND
9. TOBACCO from NORTH AMERICA
10. WOOL from YORKSHIRE for HOLLAND
11. WOOLLEN CLOTH from NORFOLK for HOLLAND
12. SLAVES from WEST AFRICA
13. LEAD from DERBYSHIRE for INDIA

 • Find out about industry in Tudor times in your locality. List goods that were produced. What evidence is there of imports?

© Folens (copiable page)   IDEAS BANK – *Tudor Times*   37

Seafarers in trouble – Ideas Page

Key element

- Communicating knowledge and understanding of the problems of overseas voyages through a problem-solving game.

Background

In the Tudor period, Spain was the super-power of the age, with an empire in South America. English merchants began to look beyond Europe and wanted some of the American trade for themselves. Adventurers such as Hawkins, Drake and Raleigh showed England's growing maritime strength.

Life on board ship was hard. Sailors had to survive brutal discipline, accidents, diseases, poor diet, the constant cold and wet and grim storms. They could be at sea for months or years – Drake's famous voyage around the world lasted from 1577 to 1580. However, a successful raid on a treasure ship could be worth a fortune.

A useful source of information about ships is *Voyages and Discoveries* by Richard Hakluyt (Penguin).

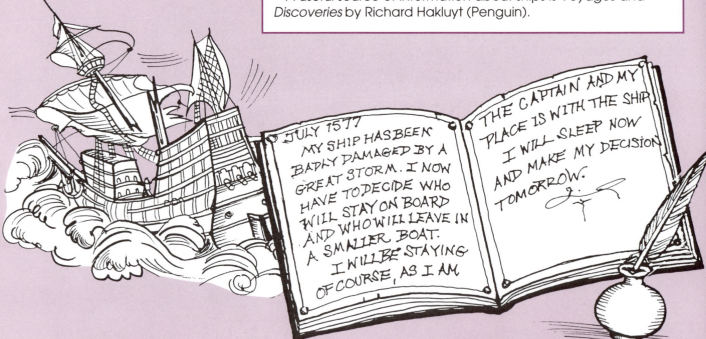

Activities

- The ship on the Activity sheet was damaged in a great storm and has been drifting for days. The navigator believes the nearest land is 500 miles away. The captain has decided to send a smaller boat out to try and reach land. If those left on board can save the ship, they are more likely to survive. But if the ship sinks, then those in the small boat are more likely to survive.
- Ask the children to imagine they are the captain, who must decide who stays and who goes. They should cut out the crew figures and glue them on a large chart with two columns: 'Stay on ship' and 'Go on boat'. (Or they could draw a boat and a ship and stand the figures on these.)
- Use this game as a starting point for 'Exploration overseas'. Discuss the preparations necessary for a long voyage. The children could pretend they are quartermasters, responsible for making a list of essentials.

Links to writing

- Ask the children to keep a captain's log, dated July 1577. They could spread the entry over several days, describing how they came to their decisions.

Key questions

- What were the jobs of the crew on a Tudor ship?
- Who were the most important crew members?

Seafarers in trouble

This English ship was on its way to attack Spanish treasure ships. It has been badly damaged by a storm.

- Choose four men to put in a boat. Those left on board have to try to save the ship. Those in the boats have to try to reach land.

50 soldiers
Help fight the Spanish.

Cooks
Look after the fire and see to the food.

Two helmsmen
Steer the ship.

Four Quartermasters,
Each in charge of a quarter of the hold.

Gunner
In charge of the cannon.

Captain
In charge of the ship.

Surgeon
Looks after the sick.

Navigator
Finds the way at sea.

Two carpenters
Repair damage and build boats.

Cooper
Checks and mends barrels.

Priest
Prays for the crew.

Musicians
Play on board and impresses visitors.

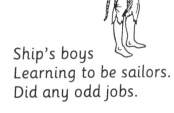

Ship's boys
Learning to be sailors. Did any odd jobs.

Coxswain
Looks after the ship's boats.

150 sailors
Look after sails and swab the decks. Can help with most things.

- Work with friends. Each choose to be a crew member of the ship. Write a speech to persuade the captain to save you.

The Spanish Armada – Ideas Page

Key element

- Describing and giving reasons for the way the events of the attack of the Armada are interpreted.

Background

England and Spain were enemies during the reign of Elizabeth I. English sailors raided Spanish treasure ships coming home from the Americas. Elizabeth had also helped the Dutch Protestants in their struggle against Philip of Spain who ruled that part of Europe. The execution of Mary Queen of Scots by Elizabeth was the last straw for Philip. Mary had been executed by Elizabeth because she was a Catholic and a rival to the English throne. Philip sent a vast fleet to attack and invade England. The Armada was not successful but the reasons for its failure are a matter of dispute. Different versions exist for different reasons.

Activities

- Explain the events of the Armada to the children as impartially as possible. A map is essential in order to describe the plan and the subsequent fate of the Armada.
- The children could complete an outline of the map first and, with the aid of an atlas, label where particular incidents occurred. Drake sent small ships, set on fire, in among the Spanish fleet at Calais. Many ships were destroyed this way.

The English commander   *The Spanish commander*

- Ask the children to go through both accounts on the Activity sheet and underline or highlight words and phrases that suggest a viewpoint rather than impartial reporting.
- Class discussion can focus upon which account seems to be the most reliable and whether it is possible to borrow from both or to place a different emphasis on the same facts. This should lead them to understand why differing interpretations occur.

Links to writing

- Ask the children to imagine they are the commander of the English force and to write a letter to their monarch explaining the reasons for the defeat of the Armada. They should then do the same from the viewpoint of the commander of the Spanish force

Key question

- The Spanish Armada – which account do you believe?

The Spanish Armada

Here are two accounts of the Spanish Armada.
- Which is the English version and which is the Spanish version?

On the 12 July the Great Armada set sail from Spain. The huge ships were like floating castles but they were not as dangerous as they looked. England had only thirty ships but they were newer and had better cannons.

The plan was for the Armada to link up with Spanish soldiers in the Netherlands (1) and then to invade England. The English fleet set sail, missed the Spanish but turned and chased them up the Channel. The Armada put in at Calais harbour (2). During the night the English sent fire ships into the Spanish Armada which destroyed many of their ships. The next day the Armada sailed north but could not pick up the Spanish army due to a huge wind that had blown up. The Armada struggled around the north of Scotland (3) and Ireland (4) and headed home. On the way many ships sank. Only 53 ships of the Armada got home (5).

It was a failure.

The greatest Armada the world had ever seen was ready. There was a total of 130 ships. The Armada was built by a genius and commanded by the Duke of Medina Sidonia, a loyal and proud man.

The Armada set out but soon ran into bad luck. A great storm damaged many of the ships. Once the ships were ready the fleet set sail again. The English were scared and terrified. When they saw the ships they were in a panic. The English fleet was smaller but its ships were slightly faster than ours.

The English did not damage the Armada but during the night they tricked the Spanish fleet into sailing out into the open seas. A terrible wind blew up and drove many of the ships on to rocks. Despite this our sailors acted like heroes. The storms did not stop and the Armada had to head for home.

The Armada was not beaten by the English ships but by the cruel, stormy seas.

 • Explain the differences between the two sources.

Sir Francis Drake – hero or pirate? – Ideas Page

Key element

- Identifying and giving reasons for the different ways Sir Francis Drake is represented and interpreted.

Background

Sir Francis Drake is often represented as a great English seaman and explorer. His famous voyage from 1577 to 1580 made him the first English person to sail around the world. To the Spaniards, he was a pirate. His voyages consisted of raids on Spanish America from which huge fortunes were made. It is estimated that almost 10–12% of England's income came from these raids. Such attacks were daring, making use of the techniques that enabled Drake to delay the sailing of the Armada (an attack on the fleet in Cadiz harbour) and the launching of the fire ships when the Grand Fleet lay at anchor off Calais a year later.

Activities

- Pupils should read the comments made by the characters on the Activity sheet.
- What are they saying about Drake? Why might they be making these remarks? The children should be encouraged to look out for possible bias.
- The children could be asked about 'heroes'. Who are their heroes and heroines? Why do they choose them? Can they think of any heroes or heroines of the past? What made them famous?
- Why do the English regard Sir Francis Drake as a hero?
- Why do the Spanish regard him as a pirate?
- Who do the children think is right? Why?
- Why would Drake's voyage around the world make him a hero? Encourage the children to consider what the ships and nautical knowledge of the world were like at that time.

The Golden Hind, *Drake's ship*.

Links to writing

- Pupils can find out more about Drake from reference books. Ask them to list Drake's good and bad points on a chart.

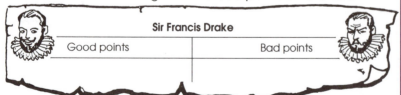

They could then sum him up. Does he seem good or bad?
- There are many other famous Elizabethan seaman – Sir Walter Raleigh, Sir John Hawkins, Sebastian Cabot, Martin Frobisher and Anthony Jenkinson. Ask the children to write about their lives and place them in a 'Heroes and Villains' gallery.

Key questions

- Would you describe Drake as a hero or villain?

Drake – hero or pirate?

- Read what people said about Drake.
- Match these to the captions.

Hero?

Pirate?

Tyrant?

Drake had my brother, Thomas Doughty, executed because he spoke against Drake. Drake said he was a traitor but he had only quarrelled with him.
(Thomas Doughty's brother)

He sent in the fire ships against the Spanish Armada, forcing them to run away.
(Sir Howard Effingham Admiral of the English fleet)

He has raided my peaceful towns in America and stolen my treasure.
(Philip II of Spain)

 Find out why Elizabeth I rewarded Francis Drake with the title 'Sir' and a grand house.

Power game – Ideas Page

Key elements

- Developing an understanding of politics of the Tudor period, particularly the power of the monarch.
- Understanding the importance of keeping in favour with the monarch.

Activities

- Provide a brief outline of the power of the monarch and how Elizabeth's government worked.
- Power Game is suitable for about four players. Enlarge the game on to a sheet of A3 paper.
- The object of the game is to get on to Elizabeth's Privy Council. In the process, players meet obstacles and advantages. They should appreciate how they are totally dependant on the patronage of the queen.
- Ask groups of children to find out about some of the Queen's courtiers and privy councillors. Each child could choose a character for a role-play. One child could be Queen Elizabeth and the rest courtiers. They should persuade the Queen that they have the qualities to be a privy councillor. They could do this by attacking the qualities of those who are already privy councillors.

Key question

- How did people try to gain power in Tudor England?

Background

In 1500, only the monarch had the right to rule. Parliament only met when the monarch told it to. However, monarchs needed the support of rich and powerful people. There were no political parties then and Queen Elizabeth chose her own ministers and officials to advise her. These people carried out the day-to-day business of the Privy Council and thus held the power in England. Elizabeth, of course, could promote and dismiss them as she chose, but William Cecil, her most important adviser, held on to his position for most of her reign.

Other prominent people in Elizabeth's court were:

Robert Dudley, Earl of Leicester. Thomas Howard, Duke of Norfolk. Robert Devereux, Earl of Essex.

Links to writing

- The children who can't get on to the Privy Council can write a job application to Elizabeth explaining why they should be included.
- Ask the children to imagine they had a manor house in Tudor times. They want the queen to visit them because this is a great honour and would help them to gain power. How would they persuade her to visit them and how would they entertain her? The children could draw up a programme of sports and activities to entertain the queen during her visit.

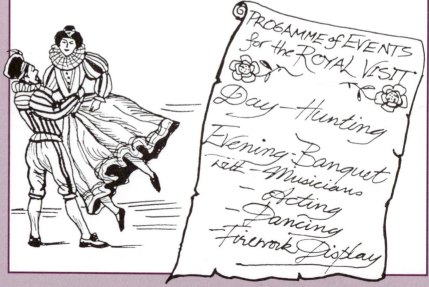

Power game

You need a dice or spinner

This game shows some of the ways people in Elizabeth I's court could become rich and powerful.

- **Start here**
- ① You marry into an important family. Move on 4 places.
- ② You catch smallpox and it takes you some time to recover. Move back 3 places.
- ④ Elected as a Member of Parliament. Move on 3 places.
- ③ You are made a Justice of the Peace. Move on 3 places.
- ⑤ You capture a Spanish ship during the battle with the Armada. Move on 2 places.
- ⑥ The queen picks you to dance with her at court. Move on 1 place.
- ⑨ One of your relatives is executed for treason. Move back 5 places.
- ⑧ You discover a Catholic plot against the queen. Move on 2 places.
- ⑦ You are sent with the English army to fight in Ireland. Move back 3 places.
- ⑩ You are thought to be a spy for Spain. Move back 6 places.
- ⑪ Elizabeth chooses you to go hunting and hawking with her. Move on 2 places.
- END.... You are now a member of the Privy Council.
- ⑬ You quarrel with one of the queen's favourites. Move back 2 places.
- ⑫ You invite the queen to stay with you on one of her royal progresses. Move on 2 places.

© Folens (copiable page)   IDEAS BANK – *Tudor Times*   45

Tudor heritage – Ideas Page

Key element

- Using Tudor architecture as a source for historical enquiry and to consider how Tudor styles have influenced later periods.

A typical Tudor timber-framed house.

Background

Many Tudor people lived in huts similar to those of medieval peasants. These have long since disappeared. The surviving Tudor buildings were mostly homes of the wealthy, or substantial public structures such as guild halls and inns.

The most popular image of the period is the black and white timber-framed building with wattle and daub infilling as shown on the Activity sheet. However there were wide regional variations. In the late sixteenth century, increasing wealth led to the 'Great rebuilding', when many older houses were renewed. Other typical elements of Tudor style include a jetty, lead lights, herringbone patterns, thatch, no foundations and limewash.

In South and East England, flint walls were common. Hand-made bricks became cheaper and were considered a status symbol, especially in eastern England. Thatch, stone tiles and clay tiles provided roofing materials.

Tall chimneys were necessary to keep sparks away from thatched roofs and many of these buildings that have since been tiled still have incongruously tall chimneys. This style of chimney persisted even for buildings that were intended to be tiled.

The different styles of Tudor architecture have been copied through the ages. The Activity sheet shows a real Tudor inn and a more recent inn built in the same style.

Links to writing

- Ask the children to design a mock-Tudor building. They should describe the purpose of the building and explain how it is similar to and different from a real Tudor building.
- The children could list the dangers of living in a typical Tudor building, for example the thatched roof would be a fire hazard and having no foundations might mean the building would be unstable.

Activities

- Ask the children to conduct a building survey of the locality, looking for examples of mock-Tudor. They can be commonly found on suburban housing from the 1920s onwards and still remain popular.
- They could sketch and record examples, such as chimneys, roof tiles and timber framing, then try to match them with any original buildings in the area, or with photographs from reference books. The examples below are based on buildings in Dunstable, Bedfordshire.

Example of Tudor design	Where found
(chimneys)	The Halifax Building Society.
(timber framing)	The Norman King public house.
(window)	The Halifax Building Society.

Key questions

- What was Tudor architecture like?
- How have Tudor styles been used by later architects?

Tudor heritage

Many buildings survive from Tudor times. Later architects have admired these and copied ideas from them. Look carefully at the pictures. Source A is a real Tudor inn. Source B is a Mock-Tudor inn, built in the victorian era.

- Make a list of similarities and differences between the copied Tudor building and the real one.

Source A: The Kings Arms, Amersham. Built in 1450.

Source B: The White Hart, Kingston on Thames. Built in 1889.

Similarities	Differences

 Look for real and copied Tudor buildings in your area. Draw and describe them.

© Folens (copiable page)   IDEAS BANK – *Tudor Times*   47

Eight ways to help ...

There are hundreds of ideas in this book to enable you to develop and extend the photocopiable pages. Here are just eight ways to help you make the most of the Ideas Bank series.

1 Photocopy a page, paste it on to card and laminate/cover with sticky-backed plastic to use with groups. Children can write on the pages using water-based pens, which can be washed off.

2 Photocopy on to both sides of the paper. Put another useful activity on the back. Develop a simple filing system so others can find relevant sheets and do not duplicate them again.

3 Save the sheets – if the children do not have to cut them up as a part of the activity – and re-use. Label the sets and keep them safely in files.

4 Make the most of group work. Children working in small groups need only one sheet to discuss between them.

5 Put the sheets inside clear plastic wallets. The sheets are then easily stored in a binder and will last longer. Children's writing can again be wiped away.

6 Use as an ideas page for yourself. Discuss issues with the class and get the children to produce artwork and writing.

7 Make an overhead transparency of the page. You and your colleagues can then use the idea time and time again.

8 Ask yourself, 'Does every child in this class/group need to deal with/work through this photocopiable sheet?' If not, don't photocopy it!